SPECIAL RESERVE

New Writing from Women in Aberdeen

edited by
Yvonne Spence

SCOTTISH CULTURAL PRESS

First published 1996
Scottish Cultural Press
PO Box 106
Aberdeen AB9 8ZE
Tel: 01224 583777
Fax: 01224 575337

British Library Cataloguing in Publication Data
A catalogue record for this book is available
from the British Library

ISBN: 1 898218 59 5

The publisher acknowledges subsidy from the Scottish Arts Council
towards the publication of this book

Printed and bound by Cromwell Press, Melksham, Wilts.

CONTENTS

iii

FOREWORD

Sheena Blackhall

'From whatever place I write you will expect that part of my "Travels" will consist of excursions in my own mind.' This was Coleridge (Satyrane's letter) making the point that not only is a reader transported to new environments when embarking on a book, but these environments will be viewed through the eyes of another, namely, the writer. In this respect, each story is a journey with the writer acting as a guide and courier.

This anthology visits many varied regions, from the Australia of Melany Stevenson's *Bush Fire*, to the Sudan and London with Leila Aboulela in *Teargas*, and off to Brussels in Molinda Black's *Breaking Glass*. Priscilla Frake, however, chooses to explore the inner landscape of the psyche and domesticity, whilst Magghi Harvey tackles the issue of PMT. Helen Donald escorts us behind the doors of a residential Old People's Home in *Isn't She Wonderful?* Other contributors introduce us to eccentric old women and nostalgic old men – *O'Flaherty's Cat* by Anne Flann is a wry cameo in the best storytelling tradition. Nor do the writers flinch from confronting the controversial – Lindsay McCrone describes awakening lesbianism, Linda Sim paints a harrowing picture of child abuse, whilst Olive M Ritch, in the story *Dolores*, explores the distress of a young girl who fears that her stepfather may have drugged and abused her.

The writers in this anthology have two things in common – they are all women, and they are all currently living in Aberdeen. And there the similarity ends, for each will guide you to her own port, to begin a unique literary journey. You will meet many memorable characters on the way – for this Anthology makes powerful reading. *Bon Voyage!*

WOMEN'S WRITING PROJECT

In March 1995, the Women's and Equal Opportunities Committee of the City of Aberdeen District Council agreed to support a proposal by Yvonne Spence to organise a Women's Writing Project in the City. This project would provide support and assistance to women interested in producing work for possible publication in a Women's Fiction Anthology, to be published during the 4th Aberdeen Women's Festival in March 1996. Additional support for the project was provided by the Council's Women's Officer and staff in the Women's and Equal Opportunities Unit.

The Council's Arts Project for Women also supported this project by running Women's Writing Workshops during the months of July and August before the closing date for submission of work. In the end, 115 pieces of work were submitted by 38 local women writers, and from these this anthology was put together with the help of a Selection Group, comprising Annie Inglis, Sheena Blackhall, Anne Stevely, Roddy Lumsden and Yvonne Spence.

The Women's and Equal Opportunities Committee's financial and other support for this project is part of their ongoing commitment to providing support for women's personal development initiatives and their aim of promoting the skills and talents of women in the City.

Leslie Brown
Women's Officer
Aberdeen 1996

THE CONTRIBUTORS

LEILA ABOULELA was born in Cairo in 1964. She lived in Khartoum and graduated from the University of Khartoum in 1985. She travelled to London to study Statistics at the LSE, and in 1990 moved with her family to Aberdeen. Her work has been published in *Mica, Chapman,* and *Left to Write*, and will be included in *Scottish Short Stories 1996* (HarperCollins).

MOLINDA BLACK was born in Shetland, attended Edinburgh University, and worked as a librarian. She now lives in Aberdeen with her husband and son.

HELEN DONALD was born and brought up in the North East, and returned a few years ago to live in Old Aberdeen. Now retired, she welcomes the chance to revive long held interests – including writing.

ANNE FLANN is a retired photo-correspondent with an expatriate American community newspaper. She has now turned to poetry and story writing to fill the gap after seventeen years of interesting events, fascinating people – and sheer hard slog. Nothing changes!

PRISCILLA FRAKE has had poems published in literary publications in the USA – including *The Sun, Visions, Inlet, The Concho River Review,* and *Orphic Lute* – and in *The New Welsh Review*, the University of Aberdeen's *Mica, Inter Alia, Oasis,* and *Ore*. She has had both poetry and fiction shortlisted in the Bridport Prize, *Northwords*, and Sutton Writers Circle Poetry competitions. Before moving to Scotland, she worked as a petroleum geologist in Texas.

MAGGHI HARVEY was born in Ayr, and now lives in Aberdeen. A few years ago a friend urged her to write. Initial faltering steps have led to more confident exploration into poetry and short stories. She is currently working in a bookstore. Her ambition is to publish something substantial before she is 40.

LOUISE E LAURIE was born in Ayrshire. She has lived in England, Wales and the Middle East where she was a secretary with the Foreign and Commonwealth Office, Jeddah. Although previously residing in Aberdeen, she now lives in West Lothian with her husband.

LINDSAY MARGARET MCCRONE was born in 1968 in Broxburn, West Lothian. She is an arts student in her final year at Aberdeen University. Her occupations and experiences since leaving school in 1984 are numerous and varied. Perhaps the most significant of these, especially in her writing of *Special Reserve*, is four years spent working as a line operator in a whisky bond. She learned about life on that factory floor. They were her formative years.

OLIVIA MCMAHON is not Scottish, but has lived in Aberdeen for 26 years. She works as teacher, teacher trainer and text book writer in the field of 'English as a Foreign Language'. She has worked in a number of places – Aberdeen College, Robert Gordon University, the University of Aberdeen, and for the last twelve years as a language trainer for Total Oil Marine. She is married with two grown-up children.

OLIVE M RITCH was born and brought up in Stromness, Orkney. She moved to Aberdeen ten years ago.

LINDA SIM is married with one small son and describes her writing as: 'Dipping my toes into the literary pool, in the hope of becoming a strong swimmer one day.'

MELANY STEVENSON was born in Morayshire and educated in various boarding schools. Her ambition was to be an actress, but her mother thought that was not a vocation for a young lady. She now works in administration with Air Traffic Control at Aberdeen Airport.

ACKNOWLEDGEMENTS

Yvonne Spence would like to thank the following:

Catherine McInerney, at the Association for Scottish Literary Studies, for advice on administration;
The members of the Selection Panel:
Roddy Lumsden, for his help in editing the final selection;
Sheena Blackhall, for the Foreword;
Leslie Brown, Liz McDonald and Joyce Douglas for supporting me with this project;
Everyone else who gave this project an enthusiastic response, helping me to keep my own enthusiasm up.

SPECIAL RESERVE

Lindsay Margaret McCrone

Lynne worked in a little corner all alone. She appeared almost to relish the solitary nature of the task she had been allocated; the building of a few palettes of heavy duty cases for an export order. She worked with a rhythmic efficiency, folding the bottom corners of the cardboard quickly and adeptly, positioning the newly formed box on the big pedal-operated stapling machine. One, two, three, four clatters of metal on card, then she spun the box off the machine and stacked it neatly on the palette.

I also worked alone that day, feeding bottles on to the conveyor belt on Line Seven. They went there through an air pump, to omit all the storeroom dust, then into the bond to be filled. An extra special whisky – a twenty-one-year-old 'Special Reserve'. Meticulous attention regarding quality checks to be taken with this order. I was obviously the wrong person for the job – 'Dizzie Lizzie' head forever in the clouds. I'd been subjected to numerous tick-offs in the past for letting too many rejects slip down the line. I'd let my life slip down the line too, flowing past fast and smooth like the glinting metal links on the belt, too busy to omit the crap.

Catherine was chatting. That was nothing new. Her voice was inaudible to me amid the sound of clinking glass and the clatter of the staple machines, but as usual she illustrated the nature of her conversation with a series of violently energetic animations. Her slim, wiry form twisted here and there, arms swinging loose and free in her baggy blue overall. The others listened intently. It was obvious the central figure of her tale was Lynne.

The supervisor suddenly glowered up from the bundle of paper and let forth a deafening 'Hoi!' Her advanced communication skills never failed to amuse me. She pointed aggressively towards Catherine's machine which had jammed up, causing all the bottles to pile up at the opposite end.

'Hoi, you!'

Catherine ran towards the menacing metal construction, thumping the big red emergency button and toying with the levers until the offending bottle was dislodged. The supervisor watched with pursed lips and folded arms as the other girls went back to work, heads bowed, hands in overall pockets.

She was watching me now so I held the empty bottles up, one by one, to the light, checking before I placed them on the belt – checking for bubbles in the glass or chips in the gold lettering. 'Special Reserve' it said. Stored away for all those years in wooden casks, piled high in a dusty warehouse,

maturing,

mellowing,

gathering strength before its eventual exposure to the elements.

My spirit once had been captured, subjugated by a cask-like surround with mould growing in the grains. And it had fermented there in that damp bedsit I had shared with Andy...

maturing,

mellowing,

gathering strength.

My attention was distracted later as Catherine strutted boldly into my line of vision, huge, dark eyes wild with effervescent energy, hands on hips. 'Saw *The Men of Texas* at the Rugby Club last night, Liz...'

Triple pelvic gyration.

'...fucking awesome!'

'Sounds excellent!'

I wished I'd gone now but I'd been quite busy recently, decorating my new place.

'What about the others? Did they all enjoy it?'

2

'Loved it. Specially Big Grace, one of the guys had her up on the stage and...'
She glanced nervously towards the supervisor's desk, via the corner in which Lynne worked. She then laid her hand on my arm and came up close to my face, the accelerated pace of her speech loaded with anger and sympathy.
'Of course, Lynne didn't get to go. Have to tell you all about it later, Liz, that old cow's watching and she's on my case.' With that she vanished as abruptly as she'd appeared.

Lynne laboured on at the same steady pace, really oblivious to the world going on around her. Her hands were young, nice, manicured nails. But the skin was weary, work-worn and red. Their inflammatory shade was echoed in the puffy circles around her wistful blue eyes. Her face was parchment pale, robbed unrighteously of its deserving youthful vigour.

Lynne's cask was fast becoming her coffin.

Catherine had once asked me, perhaps a year or so before, if I'd like to attend a 'hen night' in the city with some of the 'girls'. The 'girls' sat surrounding their enigmatic spokeswoman in the works canteen, polystyrene cups, cigarette packets, and blue tinfoil ash-trays spread out before them on the textured formica surface. They had eyed me expectantly. It was an honour to be asked, it meant you had been accepted.
'Emmm ... yeah ... okay. Sounds good'.

I'd think of an excuse later nearer the time – family wedding or something.

Andy wouldn't have stopped me from going. It wasn't as simple as that for me. Nothing with him was simple. It would always involve cruelly complex mind games and gruelling mental torture.
He'd say they were whores.
No, not say it, but imply it.
And then enforce it with some ridiculous 'proof'.

3

Preposterous gossip and small town scandal.
Women acting out of line.
Whores.
Cutting comments that hurt more than the hardest slap.
And I'd have to do everything in my power to prove I hadn't been contaminated by those 'whores'.
Prove myself worthy of being his wife.
If he could get a decent job, I wouldn't have to work in that awful place alongside those 'whores'.
Did it every occur to him, even just briefly, that I'd grown to love the comradeship they provided?
No.
The entire concept would have been completely incomprehensible to him. 'Whores' were 'whores' before they were people.

So I wouldn't go. I'd cry cooped up inside my cask, my eyes becoming red like Lynne's.

A cooper's skills is such that the numerous pieces of wood shaped together to form the barrel require nothing other than a couple of tempered metal bands to retain the golden liquid within. I pawned my rings because I left in the middle of the month and had needed a deposit for my new accommodation. I wondered if they'd known all along, like they knew about Lynne. I'd always spoken so highly of him. Kept it all inside. Like the spirit in the cask.
'Special Reserve'.
I looked at the gold lettering on the bottle. I *really* looked.
I checked for chipped lettering or bubbles in the glass.
Quality control, time to omit the crap.

MIDNIGHT WATCH

Priscilla Frake

Round with child, I drift
full-bellied, like a haunted moon
and rise through the watches of night.

My body, busy with its cells and layers,
cannot spare me certainty or wisdom.
I thought to be as tranquil

as a Renaissance Madonna
but I move jaggedly through
grief and love

and doom myself to desire.
I grope through darkness
and the clumsiness of sleep

to watch the moon, who watches me.
The width of night between us,
we share a riddle

neither one of us can answer
and glimmer palely
in our solitary towers.

LABOR

Priscilla Frake

Like a volunteer
sent out to fight a fire, I

entered the inferno:
heat: sickness: pain:
a roar and static-crackly, stupid
chatter of the midwife.
      Ignited,
womb, breast, head, all the valleys
engulfed, the hiss
bright as God.
       Walking circles dully
Voices telling me to breathe
but the smoke choking me, the pain

It ended before I died.
Now the new life nuzzles me,
a green spreads over
the blackened bloodied linen:
a fist like a bud ready to open
and a wandering blue gaze,
the blissful rain of sleep.

RATTLE, BOTTLE, HEART

Priscilla Frake

My heart was unopened,
still in its original
tamper-resistant package,
flattened under plastic wrap
and cushioned by Styrofoam peanuts,
until I handed it to you.

Now that you've ripped
it out of its protection,
I'm glad my heart
is like a rubber ball
that can be dashed against
the floor, stepped on,
or squeezed
without coming to harm

because some day
you'll learn to draw blood.
For now you teethe
on my affection,
returning my love
with your need,
and my hope
with yourself,
the fierce newness
of your midnight summons.

A WOMAN EXPLAINS

Priscilla Frake

Like you, I want to open a drawer
and find scented linen,
clean clothes folded and pressed,
neat socks.

          Instead there are
volumes of fascinating books
with cracked leather bindings,
rolls of silver wire,
and even, incredibly,
a dead mouse.

          I admire
the clean lines of your house
but I could never live there
with my wardrobe of maybes
and suitcase packed with bones.
Have pity

          and let me stay
in the ramshackle lodgings
of joy
          however untidy.

HOUSEKEEPING JOURNAL

Priscilla Frake

There's no time
I haven't stolen,
none I haven't wrested from guilt
or taken by force at the expense

of somebody's need.
Someone wants juice. Someone
wants love. Someone wants to be read to.
Even when they're gone someone wants

me to be on a committee.
As I sit, nursing this small fire
that is my own, my life,
the house stares over my shoulder.

It sits on its haunches like a desultory dog
waiting to be petted, fed, acknowledged
but I ignore it.
I survive.

DOMESTIC SKILLS

Priscilla Frake

Without cunning
the rain is depressing,
there is the work of laundry
without the pleasure of clean sheets,
the watched pot grumbles as it boils.

Cunning is needed
to survive sickness,
babies and husbands,
to learn to speak,
to learn to hold one's tongue,

to keep from being buried under junk mail.
Cunning makes the child drink up her milk,
puts dinner on the table, sends
a man out, whistling, to cut the grass.
Love, faith, and hope are all very well

but cunning transforms them into voltage,
lets them turn pistons, run the dishwasher,
and burn like filaments in milky bulbs.
A life runs screeching
like a rusty Ford

and cunning greases the wheels
and makes the remaining friction
soar like a violin, like
a sweeping soundtrack in a movie sunset
above the diminished horizon.

TUESDAY LUNCH

Leila Aboulela

Nadia is eight and she can read now. She can read the lunch menu for today, Tuesday, stuck on the door of the gym. The gym is used as a dining room during lunch. Tables with benches fastened to them cover the white lines on the floor where the children bounce balls and slide bean bags. Now as the children chatter and crowd in the queue, as the delicious smells waft through from the kitchen amidst the clutter of spoons and trays, Nadia finds it hard to believe that this is the gym room. If she were to take her skirt off right now, stand in her white shorts, run or jump, how wrong that would be, how out of place. Yet in the afternoon this is what she will be doing and there will be no smells of food, no plates, no tables and if you start to eat something right in the middle of gym, how naughty you would be. These thoughts give her a feeling of pride, she is older now, she understands the difference, she can behave in a correct way and as a blessing, as a reward, blend with everyone else, not stand apart. For this was bad behaviour, this was naughtiness, being pointed out, the centre of attention, the general disapproval for being different. You play quietly, you are alone in your own world with imaginary friends. And then if you do something wrong, even if you don't mean to, the peace is shattered, Lateefa snaps in irritation, the child's voice rises, 'Mrs Benson, Nadia broke my pencil'.

Yet knowing that she can leave the queue, that she can let go of her tray and run pretending it was time for gym, that nothing was physically restraining her, filled her with a thrill. A fear that somehow the control will slip, that she will slide to a younger, innocent age, only that now forgiveness will not come so easily as it did years before. 'You knew you were doing something wrong,' Lateefa would say pinching her arm, 'it's not that you

11

didn't know, you knew, so WHY did you do it?' Nadia is now eight and she knows that wilful disobedience is not something that adults forgive easily.

The menu is written in black in Mrs Hickson's handwriting. She hangs it up on Monday and it shows the lunches for the whole week. Sometimes before Nadia goes to sleep at night, she lies awake and tries to remember the menu for the rest of the week, listing the items one by one. Monday night is the most challenging, Thursday night the easiest. Today, Tuesday, is Chicken Risotto, Pork Pie, Mashed Turnips, Boiled Potatoes, Tomato and Nut Salad, Black Forest Gateau, and Fruit Yoghurt. Nadia knows it must be the Chicken Risotto for her and then she has a choice of the vegetables and dessert.

Nadia likes chicken. At home Lateefa buys *halal* chicken, travelling by bus every week to the Pakistani butcher in Finchley Road, and carrying four of them home in one of the green Marks & Spencer bags that she collects. Chicken Risotto, the potatoes (not the turnips, definitely not the turnips) and the cake, this is what she will take. And Mrs Hickson knows about the pork, so when it is Nadia's turn, Mrs Hickson will give her the chicken with what Nadia calls her giant fork. Mrs Hickson knows about the pork because Lateefa had told her. Lateefa had told everyone; the headmaster, who was very polite; Mrs Benson, Nadia's teacher who said that Nadia can very well read the menu and there is always a choice (a reply Lateefa found unconvincing); and finally Mrs Hickson herself who showed great interest and concern.

However, Lateefa argued later to Hamdy, if I saw one of these poor children whose crazy parents are vegetarians eating meat, I wouldn't stop him, would I? 'You would if it was your job to do so,' he said and promptly fell asleep. But just to make sure, she decided to bribe them, the headmaster, the teacher and especially Mrs Hickson. They of course never imagined they were being bribed. The headmaster got an Egyptian alabaster ash tray and an ivory letter opener. His teenage daughter, horrified at the thought that an African elephant was slain for its tusks, threw it in the attic, where it languished among jigsaw puzzles with missing pieces and headless dolls. The ash tray accidentally found its way to the school jumble sale (none of the family smoked), where Lateefa winced when she saw it and paid thirty pence to take it back home.

Mrs Benson was happier with her present, a pair of earrings with a pharaonic design, while Mrs Hickson was thrilled with her cotton cushion covers. She bought a filling for them and scattered them on her double bed. She thought they gave the room a somewhat mysterious, 'ethnic' look. 'I would love to go to Cairo one day,' she told Lateefa, 'my father was there during the war.' Lateefa told her the joke about the Egyptian village where suddenly all the babies born had blonde hair and blue eyes. There was apparently a British garrison stationed nearby during the war. But Mrs Hickson did not laugh.

It is not Mrs Hickson serving out the hot meal this Tuesday and Nadia suddenly finds herself facing a young woman she has never seen before, a woman who is asking 'Pork pie or chicken?' And to Nadia it is as if the whole room has changed or that she, Nadia, has changed. If she answers 'pork pie' or even just the 'pie', no need to say the forbidden word, just say 'pie', this new dinner lady will not be surprised, she will pick one up with the giant tweezers and put it on Nadia's plate. It will sit with the potatoes and the salad. But where is Mrs Hickson? She might suddenly appear. 'No pork for Nadia,' she will say, looking behind her shoulders and the new dinner lady will turn with a sigh, a slight irritation, 'Well why didn't you say so child,' and give Nadia the chicken.

Then Nadia asks about Mrs Hickson. The children behind her are impatient, the lady's hand is poised in the air holding the tweezers. But Nadia must ask, she swallows and speaks. 'Off ill,' the reply. Mrs Hickson has never been ill, not before, and Nadia feels there must be a pause, a time to ponder, a time to take in the newness.

Mrs Hickson is at home nursing a bladder infection, clutching a hot water bottle to her stomach, drinking water to flush the germs out of her system. She glances at the clock, 12 noon, and does not think of Nadia, or that she would be now standing

13

dishing out the meals. She only thinks *dammit, three more hours until I take the second tablet, when will these anti-biotics start to work?*

'If you don't want a hot meal, you can have cheese and biscuits with the potatoes,' the lady says, already looking at the boy behind Nadia in the queue.

'Pie,' whispers Nadia, 'I'll have the pie.'

It tastes like chicken. It doesn't taste bitter or sour. Not like the other things Lateefa forbids her to taste like perfume and orange peel. It tastes like ordinary food. Nadia pushes ketchup on it with her knife and it tastes better with the ketchup. The other children talk while they are eating, a normal day, a normal lunch hour. Yesterday Nadia was like them, but today the lunch break seems infinite, real, glittering. Tracy, Nadia's best friend, is eating the Chicken Risotto. Tracy, who on other days ate pork pies while Nadia watched and wondered. Tracy, who brings bacon flavoured crips to school and Nadia doesn't try them. Today, of all days, Tracy is eating the Chicken Rissoto. And Nadia feels a sudden dislike for her friend.

In the classroom, after lunch, it is time for mathematics. Tracy is not good in Maths, not like Nadia and while Nadia divides Tracy is still multiplying. Nadia's workbook is neat, she works quickly moving her lips as if she is talking to herself. When she finishes a page Mrs Benson checks it and stamps a picture of a boy rushing past on a skate-board. 'Keep it up', the slogan above his head says. Sixteen divided by four, twelve divided by three, fifteen divided by five. Easy. And Nadia worries a little about what she would do if the sixteen were divided by five, if the picture in the workbook showed three children with ten sweets to share among them. It wouldn't work then, they wouldn't be able to share. Nadia pushes a feeling away, a tired feeling, it is such a long time since lunch, since breakfast. But she can't think about that and can't even think of the chocolate bar she and Lateefa will share when she gets home from school.

There is a bad feeling in her chest and in her throat and she wants it to go away. Ten divided by two, six divided by three, eighteen divided by six. She is stuck, eighteen divided by six... if it was divided by nine that would have been easy but six, eighteen divided by six. Maybe it is one of those numbers that couldn't be divided like the three children couldn't share ten sweets. The numbers seem jumbled now on the page, time seems so slow. Nadia thinks she should get up, walk up to Mrs Benson bending over Tracy's red hair. When she looks my way I will speak to her, thinks Nadia and she puts her head on the workbook. It feels cool to her forehead, her forehead is damp, the black numbers on the page loom close to her, the boy on the skateboard grins maliciously and she closes her hurting eyes.

'Nadia, Nadia,' Mrs Benson's voice filters through and Nadia lifts her face up, swallows but it is too late. A gush, the sound of a tap opening, a flood on the workbook, on Nadia's lap, on Mark's pencils, a speck of potato on Brian's left arm. And on the soaked boy with the skateboard, a pink remnant of pork pie, his face still grinning through, 'Keep it up'. And Nadia keeps it up when Mrs Benson with remarkable agility positions the waste paper basket strategically in front of her. Impossible to stop, even when Brian says 'Ukk,Ukk,Ukk', and continues to say it, even with Tracy spluttering with laughter, covering her mouth with her hands, her knees clenched together, and even while Mark whines gently, 'Mrs Benson I need a new pencil.'

There is no relief. Intervals but no relief. In one of those intervals Nadia is led to the toilet. Mrs Benson is kind, helping her clean her jumper, telling her to wash her face, not angry, not shouting. Nadia is afraid she will be angry; the mess in the class – who was going to clean it and the workbook – what will happen to the workbook?

In the toilet the rest of her lunch floods out, easier now, not so thick and clogged, smoother. The red of ketchup, orange juice, lots of orange juice. And at home, when Lateefa finally picks her up and they go home, there is nothing left. She retches, her stomach squeezes itself but there is nothing left, just a dull, still pain in her muscles. A drained feeling, her body trembling.

'Get into bed Nadia, sleep and you'll feel better, I won't let you eat anything else today. Tomorrow *Insha Allah* you'll be better.' In her pyjamas Nadia feels clean, her room smells nice, the sheets are cool and comforting.

'What is it that you ate that made you so sick? What did you have for lunch?'

'Chicken,' says Nadia, her nose in the pillow, her eyes closed, and then after a while 'Mrs Hickson was off ill today.'

'What else did you eat?'

'Black Forest Gateau.'

'What's that?'

'A cake Mama, a chocolate cake.'

'It must have been the cream then. Old cream, bad for your stomach. Go to sleep now, I'm going downstairs.' Relief, an empty stomach, at last relief and sleep will come easy now.

Nadia opens the cloakroom cupboard but it is not a cloakroom any more. It is her aunt Salwa's flat in Cairo. It doesn't look exactly like Tante Salwa's flat. It is more untidy, darker, narrow like the cloakroom. Her cousin Khalid is sitting on a chair, looking out of the window. Nadia climbs into his lap and he puts his arms around her, and his cheek rubs against her chin. She asks him what he is looking at without speaking, and he shows her the busy street below, the man blowing his horn selling candy floss, another with a large rack balanced in front of his bicycle filled with pitta bread. And Mrs Hickson standing alone in front of a table covered with pork pies, a table like the ones that Nadia eats lunch on at school. The giant tweezers in her hands, a placard with the picture of the boy on the skateboard showing the price, eighteen divided by six pence. Three, says Nadia to Khalid, three pence but it is as if Khalid couldn't hear her. No one is going to buy these pies, he says.

Nadia is awake and hungry. The house is silent and dark. She has missed Children's BBC, missed Hamdy's key turning the lock on the front door. She has missed dinner. Lateefa will have told Hamdy about her being ill and sudden tears come to Nadia's eyes imagining how anxious and sad he must have been. He will have opened the door and looked at her while she slept, the way parents do on TV.

Tomorrow at school they will call her Nauseous Nadia, they will write Nozeus Nadia, NN for short. She will be hurt and ashamed. She will hope that they will forget the whole thing like magic, as if it didn't take place. But now she is hungry.

She wanders to her parent's bedroom. She can hear Hamdy snoring. Lateefa wakes up as if she was not asleep, clear and lucid and bright as if she was waiting for Nadia. She holds her daughter's cheek against her own to check her temperature. Nadia puts her arms around her and Lateefa says she will make toast and that Nadia should go back to bed.

Nadia can smell the toast, the smell made more delicious by the stillness of the night, the hunger she feels. Lateefa brings the toast with jam and they both sit up on Nadia's bed, covering themselves with the pink and orange quilt. The toast has strawberry jam on it and it is sweet and warm. Lateefa feels soft and Nadia leans against her arms, she can smell the jam and the bread. She wonders why her mother looks so beautiful now in her sleeveless cotton nightdress, not like when she picks Nadia up from school.

They giggle, it doesn't matter about the crumbs falling on the bed. They drink tea without any milk. No milk for a bad stomach, Lateefa says. The mug of tea is too hot for Nadia to hold and Lateefa must hold it for her in between sips. Lateefa has been teaching her a short chapter from the Qur'an, *Surat El-Ekhlas*, for some days now and Nadia can say it all by herself. '*In the Name of Allah, the Compassionate, the Merciful. Say: He is Allah, the One and Only. Allah, the Eternal, the Absolute. He Begetteth not, nor is He begotten and there is none comparable unto Him.*'

Lateefa kisses Nadia. 'Clever girl, not one mistake. When we go to Cairo you can show Khalid and Tante Salwa and they will be so proud of you.'

Now Lateefa takes the empty mugs away and it is time for Nadia to sleep. As sleep approaches, Nadia thinks that her mother must have cast a spell on all the wrong things Nadia should not do. Bewitched pork pies, so that even when she wanted them, they, on their own accord, rejected her.

FROM TOWN TO TORRY

Olivia McMahon

She strides out heading for home
in her red T-shirt
with something in gold written across it.
By her side, keeping up,
is a child licking a lime-green lolly,
and in the pushchair festooned with plastic bags
a baby in fondant pink.
She dodges between the cars
zipping away from the roundabout,
bumps over the rails
with dandelions growing between them
that lead from the goods yard
across the road, heavy with lorries,
to the dark harbour waters
where *The Arctic Princess* is waiting
and other ships with unspellable names.
On the left now is the wall
where someone has painted *Fight For.*
And, further on: *Job Shop Top Floor*
and *Insurance Brokers: Bland Payne*
with *in the arse* scribbled after,
next to *The Faroese Commercial Attache*
that no-one has seen.

And there are fishheads on the broken pavements,
vomit in doorways and dried bloodstains,
and seagulls everywhere splattering their whitewash.
And now *The Harbour Barber* and men tottering
adrift from *The Anchorage*
and *The Royal National Mission*
To Deep Sea Fishermen
on the corner calling them.
But she has her eyes fixed on the way ahead
on the straight line that leads
from the town to Torry,
reaches at last the bridge and the shining river
and the curve of granite climbing the hill.

DOLORES

Olive M Ritch

The words dance on the page as Dolores reads the same sentence over and over again. She looks at the books piled in front of her, queuing for attention, and wonders when she'll be able to look at them. Her prelims start tomorrow, merely a case, she tells herself, of spewing out the information in the right quantity and quality on the day but she knows it isn't that easy. Not that easy at all as the digesting has been made more difficult with *him* around – he cranks up the music when her mother is at work.

Dolores' mother works night-shift at the local hospital where she trained twenty years ago. She enjoyed wearing her nurse's uniform at first and believed she was doing something worthwhile. She felt important and liked when people said 'I couldn't do your job'. The veil of glamour was gradually peeled back as low pay and poor working conditions led to her feeling exploited. She changed from day to night-shift and became more and more weary of pounding the long hospital corridors. Dolores' mother, tentatively, mentioned her wish to give up nursing to Paul, her husband of three months, but he said they need the money for a deposit on a house.

Dolores doesn't like Paul, doesn't like the way he looks at her when her mother's not there and loathes his nose-picking habit. He examines what he's extracted as if it's a valuable catch and, then, inserts his index finger into his mouth. He chews it with a look of satisfaction on his angular face and sometimes does it at the dinner table. Dolores' mother doesn't seem to notice. She thinks her husband, who won the best salesman's award in his company last year, is wonderful and listens intently to his patter, the same patter he uses with his customers.

Dolores wishes he'd go out. She resents him always being in the house, filling it with his presence, and feels he's taking over. She can't remember the last time she had a chat with her mother, just the two of them, like they used to do. She curses him and his loud music. Then, Grandma's words ring in her ears, 'My daughter deserves a bit of happiness', and Dolores remembers promising to make an effort to make him feel welcome. She goes downstairs.

'Coffee? I've made a fresh pot.'

'Yeah, thanks,' he says looking startled. He flings the motorbike magazine he's reading on the floor and it opens at a picture of a young woman in red leather gear astride a powerful bike. He follows her to the kitchen. 'How's the studying?'

Dolores is surprised he's interested in her studies as he usually only talks about himself.

'I'm not in the mood, thought I'd have a break...'

'Yeah, right. You've been working very hard. All I used to do was sit up the night before the exam with a few joints. It worked, I passed every one.'

'A few joints?'

'Have you tried it?'

'No, never. Mum would kill me.'

'She loves it.'

'She loves it?'

'Yeah.'

'You're kidding?'

'Cross my heart...'

'Not Mum?'

'Aha!'

'But she's so straight.'

'You obviously don't know her.'

Dolores pulls at a hangnail, determinedly, and tenses her shoulders as she gives the small piece of skin a final tug. She looks at the dead skin and plays with it as she goes over what her mother has said about the dangers of drugs.

'Look, shall I roll us one?'

'Hmm...'

'It'll help you relax, you'll study better after it ... believe me I'm an expert.'

'Yeah, why not,' says Dolores, biting her lower lip.

Dolores watches him rolling the joint. With both hands he rolls it between his index finger and thumb, licks the cigarette papers, teasingly, pulls stray tobacco from either end and lights it. It looks so complicated, like an art form that takes forever to master and she gazes at him admiringly.

He draws on it greedily and then passes it to Dolores. She looks at the joint placed awkwardly between her fingers and draws timidly. She likes the smell but doesn't feel any different after a couple of drags. The paper sticks to her lower lip, burning her, and she starts to blush when she sees the soggy end stained with lipstick. She wonders why she put it on and wipes her lips with a tissue.

'Fancy a beer?'

'No, I'd better get back to Wilfred Owen.'

'*Dulce et decorum est* and all that bull-shit. Come on just one to keep me company.'

'Oh, okay. But don't tell Mum.'

'It's our secret.'

He hands her a chilled can of lager. She'd like a glass but doesn't like to go and get one, so instead wipes the top and drinks from the can.

'What do you think of the Paul Weller number that's in the charts?'

'It's okay.'

'Okay? It's bloody brilliant. Have you listened to the lyrics?'

'Yeah.'

'And?'

'It's ... it's okay.'

'You'll have to listen to the lyrics again,' says Paul as he strides across the floor to the C.D. player. 'Listen,' he starts singing along, "You do something to me, something deep inside..." '

Dolores doesn't like it any better on another hearing.

'I prefer Take That.'

Paul hands Dolores another can of lager and starts to roll a joint.

'They're not in the same league. What's the name of the one in the charts?'

'Never Forget.'

'Yeah, that's right. You were playing it the other night when Emma was around.'

'Yeah. She really likes the singer.'

'And who do you like?'

'Don't know.'

Paul watches Dolores blush and shift about in her chair uneasily.

'Listen to this, I heard it today, you'll really like it ... I suffer from mild paranoia,' grimaces Paul as he strokes the stubble on his chin, 'I don't like going to rugby matches because when the players go into a scrum, I think they're talking about me.' Paul laughs outrageously.

'That's awful, I've got a better one. What was Gandhi's first name?'

'Hmm ... can't remember.'

'Goosey, goosey...'

'Oh, Dolores ... that's really awful. Who told you that one?'

'Hmm...'

'I wish I could remember the one your Mum told me last night ... it was pretty disgusting but really funny ... something about a priest in retreat and his lurid thoughts...'

'I've never heard her...'

'She knows a lot, some, well, you wouldn't tell in polite company. She tells them in such a deadpan way, never fluffs the punch line. The lads at work blush at some of them.'

'Mum tells ... hmm ... I can't believe it ... I need a drink.' Dolores tilts her head to one side, smiles and says, 'Has the lager run out?'

'You're subtle.'

Paul places two cans in front of Dolores and puts the other on the floor beside his chair.

She opens the can and drinks thirstily from it not bothering to wipe the top. He hands her another joint.

'You're having me on ... Mum doesn't really smoke this stuff?'

'If you say so.'

'Really...'

'Like I said,' he sighs and runs his hand through his carefully cultivated Hugh Grant lock of hair, 'She just loves it.'

Dolores burps loudly, giggles then burps again.

'You're disgusting.'

'It's the lager.'

They both laugh. Empty beer cans, some crushed and split, cover the glass-topped coffee table alongside snakes of ash. Paul Weller is playing again and Dolores is singing along this time.

Dolores struggles to get up off the floor and feels light-headed.

'I'm hungry. Fancy something to eat?'

'What are you offering?' Paul asks suggestively.

Dolores doesn't hear him as she's intent on staying upright. She stumbles across the room, pausing at the door and then grabs the handle. With a look of satisfaction on her face she opens the door. Cupboard doors clatter and bang in the kitchen. She whistles tune-lessly and comes back into the living-room with egg flan and jam tarts swaying on the plate. They tuck in hungrily.

The alarm clock buzzes in the bedroom. Dolores' eyes are tightly closed as she rolls over, reaches for the clock and slaps the button fiercely. The smell of Armani lingers on the pillow and she bolts from the bed realising it's his aftershave. She feels dizzy. Sick.

Snippets of last night come back to her but she can't remember going to bed. The clothes she was wearing are like jetsam on the floor.

Her throat feels like sandpaper.

She remembers she's sitting her English prelim this morning and punches the pillow. It releases a puff of feathers.

Dolores feels shaky. She curses him and wonders what happened last night. He's been in her bed. Has she slept with her mother's husband? She cringes at the idea of his long fingers touching her and rubs the goose pimples on her arms.

He's feeding her mother, who's just returned from work, with fingers of toast dipped in egg yolk. He doesn't look at Dolores when she comes into the kitchen.

'You look awful, are you coming down with something?'
'Just nerves, Mum. I'll be okay.'
'What would you like for breakfast?'
'Nothing. Stomach's a bit upset.'
'You can't sit an exam on an empty stomach. You must have something. Toast?'
'Just leave me alone, Mum.'

Dolores stomps out of the room. She locks herself in the toilet and immediately feels guilty for shouting at her mother, her poor mother who's so trusting. They've both let her down. Dolores looks at herself in the mirror over the wash-basin and sees the physical likeness to her mother – the wide-set eyes, high cheekbones and the dimple on her chin. She hopes the likeness stops there as she doesn't want to be gullible like her, always believing what she's told. She knows he'll be comforting her mother as she sobs over her toast, stroking her hair and telling her not to worry. Her mother will be thinking he's so understanding, so wonderful. Dolores remembers him stroking her hair last night as they sat on the sofa telling jokes, silly jokes they both found funny and how she laughed at his Rowan Atkinson impersonation. Her last memory is of being held over the toilet bowl. She wonders if she passed out in the bathroom and was carried to the bedroom.

Did she, didn't she ... she doesn't know.

She feels dirty and shudders at the thought of his hands all over her. Dolores is angry with him and herself. She shouldn't have had so much to drink – so much she can't remember what happened. She wishes she hadn't offered him coffee as that's how it all started – she was just being friendly, just trying to please Grandma.

He never mentions that night, as if it hasn't happened. Dolores refuses further offers of beer and tries to ignore him leering at her.

Not knowing bothers her, keeps her awake at night.

DOLORES

A carpet of hair covers the wash-basin every morning. It's not just a few hairs and she's worried. Some weeks later she finds a couple of bald spots the size of five pence pieces and goes to see her doctor – he says not to worry.

Friends start noticing the shiny pink spots.

Soon the spots become...

Dolores wears a wig. It matches her hair colour but doesn't look real. She hates it but tries to brazen it out, pretending she's not bothered. Everyone tells her it'll grow in again, tells her not to worry about failing her exam – her mother reminds her she wasn't well that day. Everyone is so understanding, so nice but no one asks her the reason.

She thinks about telling her mother but doubts if she'd believe her.

On her sixteenth birthday she leaves a message for her on the computer screen.

> Don't be mad.
> I contacted Daddy.
> I'm moving in with him
> and Sadie.
> You've made your choice
> > now
> > I'm making mine.

> I'll call you
> sometime.

KEEPING TIME

Molinda Black

The tick of the clock
echoed click of knitting needles
in old croft houses.
Carried home by a sailor,
ubiquitous time piece
of the Islands.

Jerome and Company
New Haven, Connecticut
U.S.A.
On its front
a black glass picture, gilt edged:
a woman stands by her front door.
What does she say to the man in black suit and
hat?
Another waits by the gate.

The tick of the clock reassures,
in this townhouse.
Carried south
by new owners,
ritually wound each night
to keep Island time.

NIGHT-WATCH

Molinda Black

Miniature mouse eared bat,
in jar of apricot jam.
Spread-eagled
against glass,
grinning.
How did you get there?
Imagine
eating you by mistake
unwelcome, dastardly lodger.

My eyes narrow.
I see trees move,
creatures
swing in the moonlight.
My large body
outside, looking in.

O'FLAHERTY'S CAT

Anne Flann

O'Flaherty sat, or rather slouched, in the chair on the front sloop of the old stone cottage, puffing away at a filthy black pipe. It was not the contented puffing one sees from a peaceable man, but erratic exhumations of foul-smelling vapour, as from an ancient steam engine climbing a steep hill. There was nought in the garden that he surveyed ruminatively, but a higgledy-piggledy patch of dejected potato shaws pushing through the barren soil, like rows sown by a drunken man – which indeed they were.

By his side sat a cat, an ugly battle-scarred tom of indeterminate age. Peculiar stripes of various shades adorned his stubbly ginger fur, and an evil-looking patch over an eye gave his face the look of piratical plunderer. This did not belie his nature at all. He sat hunched, not graceful lines like most felines, but aggressively squatted, paws hunkered in towards his chest, and every now and then the claws would flex as though contemplating a forthcoming battle, or the demise of a bird. From time to time a battle-scarred eye would open like an evil wink and his tail swished to and fro as though in angry contemplation of life.

The elderly man rose stiffly and flexed massive shoulders and arms, fists clenched in tight weather-beaten knobs of bronze power. The hands of a fighting man, massively knuckled and gnarled. As he walked towards the cottage his cat rose also and stalked with the same bow-legged gait as master. A ludicrous appearance viewed from the rear. This was the sight greeting two equally elderly men approaching down the other side of the disreputable fence, which bedraggled the property rather than contained it.

'There goes O'Flaherty,' said Paddy Boyle to his companion Liam O'Reilly.

Mike O'Flaherty had been in the class above them at the school on the hill which overlooked the bay where they'd all played truant on fine summer days. There O'Flaherty had demonstrated his power over others by sheer brute force, earning him enemies from the start. None had ever been true friends, but viewed him with a frightened awe, and hidden dislike. To show one's disregard would have invited battle – so he was greeted with a spurious welcome wherever he went, an aggressive child from as early as primary one at school.

As the object of their mutual disregard exited once again from his cottage, accompanied as always by his feline companion, the two men greeted him breezily.

'Well, 'tis yersel', O'Flaherty,' shouted Paddy, while his companion chimed in ''Tis a fine evening, now, and how's yersel', man?'

O'Flaherty paused a moment before acknowledging their greeting, replying at last with a grunt.

'No better than I ought, considerin' all I've to put up with.'

Having dispensed with the obligatory formalities, the two men continued on their way down the hill to the local inn to partake of a pint or two – or even three, which they did with great regularity together. After greeting acquaintances, the two settled at 'their' table by the open doorway to enjoy their pint and a nip o' the Irish, as was usual. Another and they were in fine fettle, and downing a third they were in that state that begs reminiscences of the past – they became a trifle maudlin.

'Mind young Rosie O'Halloran with her fine flirty eyes, and a figure to torment yer very soul?'

Paddy shook his head in wonderment at the memory, and his old hands formed the time worn gesture of the male, describing the female figure – an exaggerated as describing the fish that got away.

'Aye. And 'twas O'Flaherty stole her away from out under our very noses, just as he always did – even our very marbles at school,' agreed Liam, his face screwed into a mask of sheer disgust at the memory. ''Twas ever his way to push and shove, to grab and claim the very thing ye prized the most.'

Paddy nodded agreement. 'Near stole the very girl from under me feet, and never did forgive that I married her anyway. God rest her soul, she were the loveliest creature ever did live, my Mary.'

Nodding solemnly Liam continued his tirade. 'Then there was the time ye took part in the hill race and would have won it too, only O'Flaherty tripped ye just over the brow of the hill where no one saw the foul deed,' adding with increasing anger, 'and there was the time me own darlin' Molly got knocked off her bike when that hare loupit out in her path, and she landed in the pond. On her way to meet me, she was, in her Sunday best. O'Flaherty jumpit in pretending to save her – and that pond only waist high! But she DID go on and on about him rescuing her. We had our first row then we did.' He shook his head ruefully.

'Aye,' said Paddy, 'the first o' many.' Ruminatively he proceeded to enumerate the many scraps and troubles from childhood to manhood that Mike O'Flaherty had inflicted on themselves and their friends, but adding, 'Well, I guess the man's just a fightin' man. Stood him good stead through the war an' all, if all his tales are true. An' he did win that medal.'

'Aye,' Liam butted in, 'came back to a hero's welcome with bunting and flags a'wavin'.'

Paddy, not liking the interruption, picked up the story again. 'Wounded he was at some fierce battle. Came home in an army jeep with head all bandaged and walking with a stick. You were still in the forces at the time, but I mind fine my Mary and your Molly excited and cheerin' wi' the rest. Wavin' great flags they were. The newspaper photographers were there in force and they got their picture took, one each side o' Mike. Made the national newspapers, it did. "Hero's Return" was the caption. An' all the time he was lookin' around for Rosie O'Halloran – didn't know she'd runned off with a Yank, an' him come back from the war to wed her.'

Liam nodded gravely, adding the last word, as always. 'Did sour the man somethin' terrible, it did.'

The two old mates shook their heads in unison at the great loss of the legendary Rosie. 'Aye, 'twas a terrible thing to come back to, so it was,' they both agreed, but behind the sadly shaken heads and mournful eyes lurked a gleam of sheer satisfaction at the come-uppance of their old tormentor.

'It isn't the worst he is, old O'Flaherty,' said Paddy charitably, dismissing past grievances in a burst of benevolence.

'It's that blamed cat o' his that gets me goat, or rather me pet cat,' grumbled Liam. 'It's the cause o' a' them kittens I've to find homes for. Ye'd think the brute just lies in wait for to pounce on poor Misty. No sooner one litter than she's off again.'

The two old heads nod in solemn, if drunken agreement, as the objects of their conversation pass the door of the inn, homeward bound, the bandy-legged cat, tail aloft, a mere couple of paces behind the hunched figure of his master, whose aggressive, once powerful figure is shrunken by age and rheumatism – but not in the two observer's eyes.

'Aye, I canna abide that O'Flaherty's cat.' muttered Liam.

'But old O'Flaherty's not the worst,' countered Paddy, squaring his still trim figure.

And the two old men raised their glasses in silent toast.

RED GAMES

Linda Sim

Here it is. The tiny wooden chair her mother kept. 'A family heir-loom' she called it, painstakingly created by daddy for his little girl.

So here it is, now, this unobtrusive dainty despicable little thing, squatting in the middle of her living room. A sixties relic sur-rounded by nineties youngsters. But it's the chair you sense to be the child. A pathetic tatty scrap like an orphan arriving at a chil-dren's home.

She sits on her comfy sofa and looks at it from a safe distance. For the first time in her life she really looks at it; seeing the layers of yellow, blue and red paint flaking off. It was red when he first painted it. She remembers sitting on it when it was red. She used to sit her teddy Timmy on it and play 'mummy', offering sweets and singing songs to him. But then one day daddy wanted to play a game and Timmy wasn't allowed, but could watch if he wanted. She had to sit on the chair with her hands behind her through the wooden spindles while daddy tied her hands together. Mummy wasn't there, and she somehow felt she didn't like Timmy watching even though he was her best friend. There were lots and lots of games after that, but she can't remember sitting on the blue or the yellow, only the red. Probably because part of her brain chooses not to.

She remembers the time he painted it blue with the big tin of paint. Then he painted everything of hers blue. Like an animal marking his territory.

She didn't really know why he painted it yellow. Perhaps he wanted to hide its secrets behind a bright smiling mask.

She feels a solitary tear crawl down her face and tastes its bitter sweetness, suddenly realising she feels sorry for it because she knows she's going to have to kill it.

The fire is already lit out at the rear of the garden. All she has to do is throw it onto the burning flames. She can't dispose of it along with her usual rubbish because she can't bear the thought of a dustman's child being unwittingly contaminated by its filthy secrets.

She walks towards it, picking it up easily in one hand, remembering when it was once clumsy and heavy. Then she's running quickly out of the back door, closing her eyes as she tosses it onto the yellow, blue and red blaze. The flame tongues lick it as if tasting its flavour. She thought she'd smell a putrid stench, but all she smells is burning wood and all she sees is a little girl's chair.

She wonders how she will explain its disappearance to her mother, who never understood her reluctance to give it to her daughter Sophie.

TODAY IS...

Magghi Harvey

A black day.
A seeping, aching, arguing day.
Thoughts crash within
As bitter words fly at innocent children.
Thunder in my head, lightning in my eyes.

Deep in the cloudy memories of childhood
Black trees tower and lean
Holding forbidden secrets.
Rolling thunder, piercing lightning
Force fearful tears to fall.
Rain beating on the car
Like threatening, echoing drums.
Water rushes on the windscreen
And a deep, wet night unfolds.

Heavy aching sounds ripple round
Pressing deeper into me.
Lying still, breathless
The flooding, red rivers flow
Releasing petals
Floating like dead butterflies.

EXPEDITION TO ANTARCTICA

Priscilla Frake

Big deal. Having a man isn't everything. I can manage just fine on my own. My friends ask if I get lonely at night. Maybe I do, but at least I get to do what I want. If, say, I decide to go to bed at nine, I just do it. I don't have to lecture Doug not to wake me or tell him to turn down the TV. I don't have to stumble over his work clothes tossed all over the bedroom floor.

I won't have to live in this godforsaken town much longer either. As soon as I get enough money together, I'm going back to Colorado. They have mountains there, trees, streams, lakes, scenery... anything you want. I don't know how anyone can stand to stay in West Texas. It's flat, dry, windy all the time. I want to live where there are actual seasons, not summer for nine months of the year, and I want my kid to know about winter and snow. When I was little I loved snow, especially when we'd get a really big storm that would drop several feet of powder. I'd plough through drifts, pretending I was Commander Scott trying to find the South Pole. Wander around till I was almost blind from the whiteness of it and numb with cold. I liked the feeling that I was all alone, that no one would hear me if I shouted. I'd shout things I would never say, in the hollows formed by snow banks and rocks.

I called Marge a while back and told her my plans. I'm taking the kid and splitting. Vamoose, I said. I always liked the sound of the word vamoose. Sort of lonely and magical, trailing off at the end like a train whistle.

'You've been talking about it for a year. So what?' she says.

'I mean it. This time I'm serious. You want to hear what he did?'

'Tell me,' says Marge. I can hear her lighting a cigarette,

settling down in her chair. My stories are always good. 'Took Danny out shooting.' I start chipping at the linoleum of the kitchen table with my fingernail. 'I was out shopping or I would've stopped him. He *knows* how I feel about guns. And Danny's only seven. Seven years old, goddamn it, too young to join the freaking NRA. He could have blown Danny's head off or something. Imagine the Headlines: WOMAN KILLS HUSBAND WITH FRYING PAN AFTER SON DIES IN SHOOTING ACCIDENT.'

In the background, I can hear Marge murmuring in sympathy. She's good at that, it's why I call her first. She always agrees with me. Not that any of my friends have much good to say about him. Sometimes I even find myself defending him in front of them, as if I could switch to his side if I wanted to.

'So how about that job,' I ask. 'Do you think I'll get it if I apply?'

'Five bucks an hour doesn't amount to much.'

'It's something until I get on my feet,' I say. I don't ever expect my jobs to last. So far, they haven't.

We hang up and I put on my best jeans and go to the Dairy Queen and apply. I get the job easy enough, too, which shows him. He said they'd want someone with experience.

The thing is, he keeps calling me. I talk while I fry burgers, keeping an eye out for the manager. Sometimes I get orders confused after I hang up and Carmen, who works the front, gives me the evil eye. She says I'm lucky I don't have to face the customers when I've screwed up and given them a chilli burger instead of one with cheese. She says I have a real talent for mixing up orders on the worst customers – the scrawny old ladies who come here after church on Sundays. 'You don't have to listen to them yell,' she says.

The cold snap hits me unprepared. I expected to be in Colorado by now, where it's colder, but the wind doesn't blow as much. Not like this wind, which sweeps down across the plains from the north. It even snows, amazingly enough, a light powdery snow, too fine and light to have any fun with. Danny wants to go outside, so

I get our parkas out of the back closet and wrap us up in scarves and mittens and woollen hats. People around here don't know how to dress up in cold weather.

We set out across the vacant field in front of the apartment complex where we live. The snow is blinding now that the sun is out, but there's hardly enough for us to make tracks in. I think about Antarctica, how cold and lonely it is there, with cliffs of ice sculpted by the wind. You can get lost in those ice ridges, they say. Walk around and around, like being caught in a maze. Maybe never get out. The sun goes behind some clouds and it goes flat and cold all of a sudden, too cold to stay out any longer. I scoop up Danny in my arms and bury my face in the fake white fur around the hood of his parka. His warm face is inches away from mine and I can hear his raspy little breathing. His nose is clogged again. I tell him we're going home.

BUSH FIRE

Melany I Stevenson

The day began unbearably hot. It was no good when the temperature was continually over forty degrees Celsius for such a long
time. Even with air conditioning the house never felt cool, you
couldn't sleep, you became lethargic and tempers were beginning
to flare. The Kookaburras still screeched but they seemed to be
quieting down, the grey and pink Gallahs slowly padded about in
the shade of the trees catching flies and bugs in the yellow stubby
grass. On reflection, Blue hadn't seen so many dingoes about
either, and a silence seemed to be creeping over the outback.

As he drove his battered Nissan 'ute' down the red dust track
towards Tukanarra, he noted that there didn't seem to be the
normal amount of kangaroos or wallabies either. It was only 5 a.m.
and they should be feeding in the scrub. After driving for over an
hour, he stopped the 'ute' outside a small house with a fuel pump
in the yard and jumped out of the cab. Pulling open the fly door of
the house he shouted, 'George, get up you lazy bugger you've got
a customer,' slammed the door behind him and walked back to his
vehicle.

After a few minutes an overweight short built man in dirty vest
and shorts stumbled out of the house rubbing his eyes.

'God damn it Blue, don't you ever sleep?' he asked. Walking
over to the fuel pump he continued, 'Is there a purpose to this visit
or are you going walk about again?'

'Nope,' Blue replied. 'Going up to Newman and then to Port
Hedland, got a job there.'

'You in proper job,' George said laughingly, 'this I don't
believe. When do you start?' he asked.

'Tomorrow, maybe Thursday, when I get there,' Blue replied.

39

'Better get up there fast, or be no job waiting. What do you want a real job for?' he asked.

'Pension,' was the answer.

Blue loaded up the jerry cans in the 'ute' packed them between cages and sacks, got in his vehicle and drove off.

George stood watching him go down the dusty track. Scratching the stubble on his chin he mused, can't imagine Blue in a job again, opened the door to his house and walked into the darkness. Blue had been employed by the government, no one could remember what exactly he did, but it was something with the importation and exportation of animals. Animals were his life. He had given up his job a long time ago and now made a living from time to time being a guide to TV and film companies working in the bush and outback. George couldn't understand why he was going to work for an iron ore mining company, it didn't add up. Shrugging his shoulders George opened the refrigerator door, grabbed a can of coke off the shelf and walked towards his bed.

Blue drove on along Route 95 towards Nannine. There he would stop before going to Meekathara to stay with his old university friend Steven. They had been friends since the early 1960s and had kept in contact. He enjoyed his friend's company and debates, he was looking forward to a few beers with him. He drove up the main street of Nannine, stopped outside the general store, got out of the cab of the 'ute' and wiped the sweat off his face. Another scorcher of a day, the weather had to break soon he thought. Before he entered the general store he could hear the radio blaring away. How old Bert could listen to that noise he would never know – maybe that was why Bert was going deaf. The garbage some of those presenters spoke was enough to wear out your patience never mind your ear drums. Blue liked his own company, was comfortable with the sounds of the outback and enjoyed feeling the earth beneath his feet. You could learn a lot by looking at the ground, tracking and being able to watch the lizards before their camouflage would blend them into the scrub. With almost ten years of living in the outback, he was beginning to really understand the Aboriginal philosophy and legends.

After collecting his mail and walking towards the local 'hotel', he entered and ordered breakfast. While eating breakfast he caught up with the gossip. A group of sheep shearers ambled in and strode over to the bar. It was almost 11 a.m. when he left the hotel and upon entering the street again he felt the heat of the sun, but the heat had changed, there was a stirring in the air. As he walked back towards the store, dust was beginning to blow from his footsteps.

Just as he was reaching the store tall Tom Darcy came running out.

'Go back to the pub,' he shouted, 'get everyone out – bush fire at Annean Junction – everyone needed.'

Blue jumped into his 'ute', started the engine and roared down the street blowing his horn as he went. People came out to see what the fuss was. Leaning out of the window of the cab he shouted the news, and within a couple of minutes he had five sturdy men in the back amongst the cages and sacks, two more in the cab beside him. It was about fifty miles to Annean, the 'ute' flew along the highway and when they reached the dirt track the vehicle seemed to have a mind of its own as it bounced along in the direction of Annean. By the time they had reached the turn off, the wind had picked up and some animals were running about as if they had gone crazy, the men could see the fire up at the Junction.

They were met by men wearing scarves around their mouths and noses, hats on their heads which seemed to give very little protection from the sun. The heat of the sun and fire was excessive, almost making breathing difficult. Members of the State Police were there and someone said that the army had been called in. This was a bad fire Blue realised. Water would be scarce as the creek had dried up weeks ago, and the bore holes here wouldn't be able to bring up enough of the sulphur smelling water. Men were digging ditches, others beating the flames with mesh brooms, but the wind kept blowing and the fire burning. Sometimes the fire would jump from one place to another, it appeared to fly through the air, it ran up and down the scrub bushes and trees but would not subside.

Daylight became dusk, but the men didn't notice because of the thick acrid smoke. Women came with an unlimited supply of tea, coffee, soup and stew. The fire raged on. During the night a bright orange glow could be seen for miles. No one had noticed that Blue had disappeared, it wasn't until morning that someone asked if he had been seen.

After a few days the fire burnt itself out and left a large black scar on the earth. Several species of plant require bush fires to germinate their seeds, before the wind blows them away to land on the hot earth, and within several weeks green shoots could be seen sprouting through. Another cycle had begun. At the beginning of the following week, a tropical storm blew through, bringing strong winds and lashing rain. The creeks couldn't cope with the rainwater, and widespread flooding occurred until the water softened the earth and soaked through.

On the Friday morning, George was woken up by someone shouting and banging his front door. Rising from his bed sleepily, he located his shorts and slowly pulled them on, zipping them up as he reached the door. As he entered the shadow of the building he got a shock. 'Blue, you old bugger, what are you doing here?' he asked. The man turned and smiled. As George approached the 'ute' he noticed the cages held various species of animals.

'You been trapping again?' he asked.

'Nope,' was the reply, 'taking them back, they were hurt in the fire, better now,' Blue explained.

'You never went to Newman,' George said.

'Nope,' Blue replied. 'Going tomorrow.'

George shook his head and continued to refuel the vehicle and cans, wondering if Blue would ever get as far north as Port Hedland; he doubted it somehow. The only way he would go there was if some animals were in danger, but knowing what a desolate place it was, even if by the Indian Ocean he couldn't see Blue living there – maybe over at Dampier where the beach was nice and a lot of marine life, but Blue was an outback and bush man; it was his life.

CARRA'S SMILE

Lindsay Margaret McCrone

Mascara always smudges when applied as the finale of a greatly rushed make-up routine; bottom lashes all clogging together, looks like spider's legs. A bit unrealistic and overdone, a bit seventies, like one of those chicks from Abba. What can I say, Carra?
What can I tell him?
Where are my cotton buds?
Shit! He'll be here in five minutes. Carra would have had it all prepared by now, what to say. Word for word she'd have it, perfected and polished. Practised and prepared for performance; like a Shakespearean soliloquy.

But I can't think, hell, I can't think what to say. The truth? Just don't fancy him, really, no chemistry there.
But you can't say things like that to people, it's not nice, shatters their self-confidence.
Maybe I could put it off for now, just go along with...
No, definitely not.
I can't stand the thought of him...
Close to me.
Kissing me.
Touching my hair ... I can't ...
Think, for god's sake! What can I say?

I've always suffered from this severe inability to think anything through, often doing things just because they're expected of me. Or making decisions impulsively, spontaneously, on the 'spur of the moment'. Carra refers to this characteristic as the 'romantic streak' in my nature. Carra weighs up the 'pros and cons' of a situation in her head, she psychoanalyses people.

43

Two minutes to eight. He was late last time. Perhaps I have time to
run out and phone Carra; ask her what to do...
And her smile appears before me, broad and calm. Yes. Carra will
advise me what to say.

He's here.
One step from the fucking phone box, and his car grinds to a halt
in the space outside my block.
Descends nonchalantly from vintage Landy, palm placed proudly
on the pristine paintwork, prized possession. Flicks hair back from
his face, retrieving something from an inside pocket...
An HMV carrier.
CDs.
Anticipating some sort of 'cosy night in?'
Threads of aggravation unravel at a quickening pace inside me;
how dare he just assume.
Assume that I don't want to go out somewhere. Assume that I ulti-
mately want to be forced into some private space with him.
He's treading dangerous ground.
I feel threatened; protective armour emerging like a hedgehog's...
Keep the head.
Don't overreact.
I'll play it cool. I'll make assumptions too, like we ARE going
out...
'Hiya! Bet you're surprised I'm ready and waiting for a change!
Are we going into town then? Or just up the Black Bull?'
'Oh...'
Smile evaporates gradually. Glances down sideways through his
hair, at the little black and red bag in his grasp.
'You want to go out? I thought we might stay in and listen to some
sounds. I got the new Monster Magnet CD, thought you might
want to hear it.'
You know what thought did.
And who the fuck are Monster Magnet anyway?
'I hate staying in. I need a drink. And anyway, my room's a mess,
I don't like people coming in when my room's a mess.'
I don't like people coming in my room when they haven't been

invited.
I don't like people just presuming they are welcome either.
I don't like people violating my personal space.
'Sorry. I just thought ... Will the Black Bull do then? I'm a bit short of juice for getting into town.'
Looks a bit disgruntled; a wee bit put-out.

The Black Bull has one of these gigantic screens, and all the regulars are watching the football on Sky. Ken places his hand on mine.
Feels uncomfortable. Horrible, almost.
He smiles into my face. He has too much gum showing. I attempt to block out my repulsion in a last desperate attempt to be 'normal', try to find him attractive as most other girls do. But I can't.
It's there.
I feel it.
It exists.
Withdraw my hand, using it to lift my glass.
An atmosphere is developing, stale air, sourer tasting with every breath...

I'd been here with Carra yesterday, and her hand on mine was white and warm. Her face was comfortingly close, intense dark eyes locking mine in their direct gaze. She said 'I know exactly what you mean, Shannon. I don't think he's your type.'

I always drink too fast when I'm nervous. 'You can't half knock them back,' he comments.
Perhaps I'm giving the impression that I'm some sort of nut-job alcoholic, with any luck he might develop a dislike to this seedier side of my nature. 'Yeah,' I say, 'I want to get pissed.' Concerned and woeful expression. 'What's wrong Shannon? There's something wrong, isn't there? It's me. Isn't it?'

And he looks even sadder now and more forlorn. But I've seen it all before, it's pathetic really, manipulative tactics. They think that by gaining your sympathy you might be persuaded to change your mind.

'I knew I'd end up getting dumped. Have I been too heavy? I knew I shouldn't have shown my feelings, but, well, I can't help it, can I? I can't help how I feel. Or is it the age thing? It is, isn't it? You think I'm too young, think it's just infatuation. It's not though, just give me the chance and I'll prove it. Or is it someone else? Please say it's not. Please say it's not Steve, I couldn't handle that...'

And he shakes his hair, his voice raised to an emotionally charged whining pitch. In his present impassioned state, I conclude that he does not have the capacity to comprehend an explanation concerning sexual chemistry. What is it, after all? Do I understand it myself? My head hurts; I need the comfort and reassurance of Carra's smile, I feel SHE would understand.

'It's Carra' I say.

'Carra'.

He's calm now, looking at me with a pained disbelief in his beady green eyes. Shot into submission like a bird of prey. Dying eyes, poisoned pellet puncturing his utopian conceptualisation of boy/girl romance. A curve ball from the blue.

Maybe I've known all along; known that type of set-up was not for me. Perhaps I've loved Carra much longer than I'd realised, because I've just realised. Here and now. With Ken.

The problem is that I've never thought things through, I do them just because they're expected of me.

Then I realise.

Suddenly.

Intuitively.

Must be the 'romantic streak' in my nature.

SWANSEA NIGHTS

Louise E Laurie

We were a group of eighteen year olds,
awkward, gawky. Forever giggling
at something and nothing.
Huddled together by a comon factor,
forming fickle harems
ripe for the picking.

We were weekend Babycham drinkers
intoxicated by bubbles of discovery,
naughty thoughts, breathless whispers.
Flirting with butterfly eyes,
wearing mini skirts with maximum effect
in star spangled dungeons of mystery.

We stood for hours and hours
decorating smoke-filled trendy bars
duly deafened by seventies sounds:
T-Rex, Gary Glitter, Amen Corner
all cornering the market
with their psychedelic powers.

We allowed dim corners to tease us
with silhouettes of sophistication
but our tedious self-consciousness
still lingered, clung
as we danced around
our man-made barricade of bags.

Champagne days
of our Swansea nights.

EARLY MORNING CALL

Louise E Laurie

A flurry of feathers descended
in seconds
eagle eyes had spotted a pinprick
of entry
now a gaping hole of black plastic.

Eggshells, teabags, chicken bones
laid bare
on pristine suburban lawns
for frenzied inspection
no pecking order here.

My city ears had grown deaf
to seaside chatter
to wailing, clamouring, raucous gulls
in full inconsiderate throttle.
My early morning call
by courtesy of nature.

CHEZ MAGGIE

Louise E Laurie

In the old part of town
dwarfed by concrete flyovers
in an area not quite run down
although home to stray dogs,
lived my friend Maggie.

She was always dressed in brown
with tatty, tartan pom-pom slippers,
sported extravagantly arched eyebrows
to do justice to unruly hair
and vermilion slashed lips.

I loved to visit Maggie
in her stuffy lean-to kitchen.
I didn't see eccentricity
when I was thirteen.

Careless over housework
immune to months of dust
she'd simply shrug her bony shoulders
and wring her wrung-out hands
as not one to make a fuss.

We shared many secret jokes
as we gorged on sticky, sickly buns.
Sang pop songs out of tune
when her soft Welsh lilt
was often hijacked by raucous laughs.

I didn't see stark poverty
I didn't see dependency.
I only saw an open heart,
an open house, an open door.

I have since sampled
cordon bleu cuisine
under domed chandeliers
but nothing compares
to hospitality chez Maggie.

BREAKING GLASS

Molinda Black

Sally was startled awake by a loud knocking on the bedroom door. She sat up, immediately alert.

'Relax,' said John. 'It's just breakfast being delivered, not "Nightmare on Elm Street".'

He bounded out of bed like a golden retriever and took in the laden tray, placing it on the table by the window. He did a mock bow.

'Madam, your breakfast is served.'

Sally still sat bolt upright, staring at the wall. John stroked his chin and looked at her for a moment before moving across.

He put both arms around her and she leant her head against his neck.

'You're like a coiled spring, woman.'

'Mark will have read the note. I've actually done it. I've left him.'

'Well, you're not going to sit around here brooding all day. So out of the bed with you.'

He pulled back the duvet and dragged her to her feet, slapping her bottom as she went to the bathroom.

While she was away, he bent down and took a bottle of champagne out of the mini-bar. He filled two glasses, humming as he poured.

Sally washed her hands and looked at herself in the large steam-proof mirror. I didn't think it would be like this. I should have told him face to face. So cowardly.

John appeared at her side and put his arm through hers.

'Don't they make a lovely couple? Come and have a drink, that'll cheer you up.'

Sally picked up her glass, sipped, then set it down again.

Carefully. John looked over at her, eyebrows raised.

'I was thinking of the last argument I had with Mark. He just refused to discuss the problems we were having and eventually I saw red. I threw a crystal glass at the kitchen door.'

'Well, you're not going to make a habit of it are you?' John said, and put the glass of champagne back in her hand.

John knew Brussels well. He knew a lot of cities well. He was an international businessman and had the portable phone and laptop computer to prove it. Naturally, he knew the most interesting places to go. Sally, in her present frame of mind, was happy to be led.

The Brussels Hilton was surrounded by expensive boutiques for the seriously rich. Sally felt slightly ill at ease in her non-designer clothes. Smart women with rapacious expressions, laden with chic shopping bags, averted their eyes as they strolled past the North African beggars who sat on the pavement.

'Right. First stop, the Antique Fair. I picked up a great bargain the last time I was here. You know, the gilt mirror in the dining room?'

Sally was not particularly keen on antique markets but said nothing, just put on her sunglasses and tried to enjoy the atmosphere of a new place. Normally, she loved the heightened perception that travel gave you. Mark hated to go abroad. He didn't like flying, just wanted to potter around at home if he had time off.

When John had tired of the bric-a-brac, they headed towards the garden of the Petit Sablon. As they sat on a bench, holding hands, a wedding party entered through the top gate and walked down past the statues towards the little lake. The assorted family and friends were in good spirits, laughing and joking with each other. The bride and groom, however, seemed ill at ease and nervous in their finery. Only at the command of the photographer did they venture a smile. Two pageboys ran round the lake, bearing the wedding rings on red velvet cushions. The rings seemed to be securely attached by lengths of ribbon.

'They don't look very happy, do they?' said Sally, releasing John's hand for a moment.

'She's so fat, she's nearly bursting out of that dress. No wonder she's uncomfortable,' he said.

It was like watching a play and Sally was sad when they moved off. She thought back to her own wedding day and the hopes and dreams she had then. How had it all gone wrong?

Next stop – the Musée de Beaux Arts. John decided to look at the Modern Art Collection. He had recently started to collect paintings.

'I'll give that a miss, I think,' said Sally. 'I'd quite like to see the Breugels.'

Mark had a postcard in his study of the Fall of Icarus. According to the guide book, it was in Room 31. She walked purposefully through the crowded rooms, ignoring all the other paintings until she found it. 'About suffering, they were never wrong, the old masters...' Mark was always quoting poetry. He was an English teacher and he was passionate about literature. She could never get into all that. This picture and the poems really meant something to him though. She stood in front of the picture and looked at the two legs disappearing under the waves. The other people going about their business, unconcerned. She experienced that recurring pain in her stomach. Somehow she must try to relax a little. Mark, why did you have to be so boring all the time? Never talking. Always sitting with your nose in a book.

That last evening, when she had broken the wine glass, she had crept downstairs to clear up the mess. It had already been done. All that remained was one little shard glistening like a diamond. She picked it up carefully and put it in the bin. Through the kitchen window, she could see Mark, on his knees, weeding in the twilight. He paused briefly and pushed his hair back off his forehead. There was an air of defeat in the slump of his shoulders. For a moment, she had a strong urge to go out and hug him, but she resisted and went back upstairs. She had packed and gone to John's the next morning when Mark was at school.

They had a pre-dinner drink at an outdoor cafe in the Grand-Place. John was on the mobile phone for the tenth time that day.

'Sounds good to me, Peter. Get them to agree to that and it's a done deal. Yes, just enjoying a day off before the meeting tomorrow. Showing Sally the sights. Ha Ha.' He stroked her thigh. Sally edged away slightly, she had been enjoying the architecture of the square. Impressive. She sipped her white wine and looked again at the name of the cafe, 'La Rose Blanche'. The white rose. Another of Mark's quotes. 'The little white rose of Scotland would break your heart', or something like that. He used to say it to her when she was angry with him.

John had made a reservation at a fish restaurant on the Quai des Briques.

'Pricey, but the company's paying.'

Sally wasn't fond of fish. On the way there, they passed an old church. Pink rose bushes clustered at the side, their scent perfuming the evening air. Sally leant over the low wall to inhale more deeply and was confronted by the sombre sight of a dead pigeon lying on the grass, its glazed eyes staring up at her. She gripped John's hand.

'Careful. You don't know your own strength,' he said and kissed her.

Sally became increasingly morose as the level of the wine bottle fell.

'I shouldn't have left like that. Just a note. He deserved better.'

'Why did you come if you were going to be so bloody uptight? Could you not lighten up a little. Laugh at life?'

The waitress poured more wine, hovered nearby.

'What is it that you want Sally? Do you have any idea at all?'

'I was unhappy with him and now I'm unhappy here with you.'

'I don't believe this. You've been wanting to leave him for months. Well, haven't you?'

Sally almost choked on a red mullet bone. She had to swallow furiously, eat dry bread, drink. A hard lump passed down. Her gullet felt grazed.

John picked the bones of his Ostend sole clean. The bones were hard and firmly attached to each other.

John unpeeled a toothpick and proceeded to use it. He waved

away a flower seller who approached their table.

Back in the hotel bedroom John got ready for bed. Sally listened as he urinated aggressively. 'Mannekin Pis,' she thought and sniggered. They had seen the famous little statue earlier in the day. She changed her mind about taking off her clothes. John started to brush his teeth, an operation which would last for some time. She picked up the key and left the room.

In the Lobby Bar a man played the piano. At his side stood a young woman, singing and playing the violin. They looked at each other a lot and smiled. Sally wondered if their rapport was genuine or merely for the benefit of the audience. She sat down by herself on a two-seater sofa, ordered an Amaretto liqueur and leant back to observe her fellow late-night drinkers.

A fat Canadian with the UN Peacekeeping Force kept bustling up to the entertainers and making requests. A pair of decorous Japanese grinned at each other. A tall skinny man looked sadly into his pint glass and over in the far corner an elderly couple held hands and tapped their feet in time to the music.

Sally went back up in the lift, grimacing at herself in its mirrored walls. She entered the room quietly, noticed that the curtains were not drawn. The window was open wide. As she crossed the room, John sat up in bed, swinging his legs out.

'Stop. Wait right there,' he said.

He stood behind her and put his hands over her eye. Guided her towards the window. Pushed her head out into the fresh air.

'What the hell is going on?' Sally shouted.

He took his hands away and she saw the new moon.

'It's bad luck to see it through glass,' he whispered, stroking her back.

'It's too late,' she said. 'I saw it from the taxi on the way home.'

ISN'T SHE WONDERFUL?

Helen Donald

I cannot tell night from day.
If I am in bed
It must be night.
I know the sounds of dawn.
The birds don't sing any more,
Instead, vehement women
Crash and bang
In the corridor.
They sweep and brush and rattle
Their buckets.
Then 'Time you were up.
You'll need help with
Your stockings.'

My slow zimmer waits for me.
I grasp its steadying handle,
String bag in its place.
All the things that matter
Are safely there.
The lift is impatient with me.
Closing its expanding gate
Is hard, as you face inwards.
They say you hear a click, then
Press the button.
Off we jolt, down we go,
Me and my zimmer.

The dining room is dark,
Everything is dark.
I count the paces to my place.
There is a smell and a noise.
The chattering girls never let us linger.
As they wend the smell
Of cooking wafts.

Afterwards, I make for my chair
Not an easy chair.
I sit bolt upright.
Someone came to visit me today.
Did I remember to be a nuisance
And ask for a jar of Vanishing Cream
From Boots? I keep drifting away;
I dream.

I dream of the days I was
Part of the world.
I even sailed round the world.
In far away New Zealand
I sampled water from a spring.
No one told me until
Afterwards that it was
'The spring of everlasting life.'
A foolish mistake, the fault is mine.
'Next birthday she'll be 99'
I think I heard them say.

TEARGAS

Leila Aboulela

She held the day up with pegs. Five pegs. And when she was away morning billowed into afternoon, into night, unmarked. When she was away Majdy no longer found her prayer mat folded on the bedroom floor, the old *tobe* she used for praying dropped over it in a coiled heap. She had put them away in her side of the cupboard, folded them neatly on top of each other to await her return. And they remained there unwanted, unnoticed until one morning when he came across them as he prepared to go out and they stirred in him an old childish sense of exclusion, of being left out, like a pleasure he had wilfully denied himself and now forgotten the reasons why.

She had left the *tobe* and the mat behind, they did not need to make the trip with her to Khartoum. In Khartoum there were plenty of other mats. Mats with worn faded patches in those places where people pressed their foreheads and stood with wet feet. Her mat in London was new and locally bought. He had bought it for her himself when she first arrived. Had made the trip specially to the Central Mosque, and it was his first time as he had never been there before, to get her the prayer time-table, the mat and ask which direction the Ka'ba was. To his amusement they sold him a compass with an arrow which pointed towards Makkah.

You have been here a *whole* year without praying? she had reproached him. And Fridays, the Friday prayer? I have classes that day, he had replied and her answer was quick, without hesitation. *Miss them.* And then for the first time he had called her stupid. Don't be stupid Sumra, he had said, where do you think you are? Then to soften the harsh words, for he was aware of her hurt on that day, her first day in this new city, her first encounter with the grey skies, the constant swish of cars on wet roads, he said, It's not as if I am finding the course so easy that I can play truant. But she had switched off by then and was not listening, was thinking of how to adapt herself without a mat, without knowing the exact times for dawn, for noon. And in those early days, before he went to the Central Mosque, she used a towel, the unreliable look of the sky to gauge the times and, with his help, geography to guess which way she should face. When the compass arrived, they congratulated themselves on getting the direction nearly right.

When she went to Khartoum that summer, it was like the year he had spent alone in London before they got married. The days drifting together, no reason to come home in the evening, all around him too much quietude. Without her he was not sure how to organise his day, to work at home or at the library, to work late at night or wake up early in the morning. He knew it did not matter either way but that early sparkle of liberty which had characterised the first days of her absence, that feeling of relief, of a responsibility shed, soon faded away and freedom hung around him stale and heavy.

Yet there wasn't anymore that feverish tension which existed when he first came. Tension and the nagging fear of failure. He had passed his qualifying exams after all. After banging his head against books, working the proofs again and again, copying curvaceous lambdas, gammas and sigmas from the blackboard and into the whirling mass of his dreams, he had passed. Now a Ph.D., though daunting, at least seemed feasible.

When he had first arrived, he discovered holes in his knowledge. Patches of blankness, areas of shaky foundation. And back home he had thought himself amazingly clever, a mathematical jinn who would dazzle London's academic elite. They would wonder how someone with his abilities could emerge from the darkness of Africa. They would honour him, welcome him. Instead he found himself to be a product of an educational system that was too poor to catch up with developments. Money bought computers, the latest textbooks, up-to-date journals and motivated lecturers. To be clever was not enough. And so to fill these holes he had to work, read, unfurl the mysteries of formulae in textbooks to catch up with the other students. A mixed lot, Greeks and Irish and Spanish, other Africans and South Americans those he felt an affinity to, the aura of the Third World bound them. In their eyes he saw his fear, and turned away to avoid their furtive message, the shameful whisper, *I am not going to make it*, lest it contaminated him and he was not immune.

And the outside world did little to help him. Khomeini, Saddam Hussein, reckless extremists who held Western hostages, they were like grotesque distant relations impinging on his new life. Caricatures who delighted in embarrassing him. Time and time again he was rendered apologetic, calling them mad, seeking to disassociate himself from them.

The University's handout for overseas students warned him not to waste the doctor's time if he had a cold. Colds were part of British life. It told him that overseas students tended to worry about their family and friends back home caught up in political unrest, and so their work suffered. It told him he would find it difficult to do his own research because he was culturally disadvantaged. His culture taught him never to question his father, his elders, his guru. (He did not understand the word 'guru', had to look it up in the dictionary, then had to look up the word 'facetious' to understand the definition of 'guru'.) And research was all about questioning, about challenging established knowledge.

He had no guru, did not know of any gurus. But before he could begin to tackle that cultural inferiority which stood in his way, he read about how fortunate he was to be a member of such a liberal institution which was open to all ideas and inclinations. In the handbook he found that by virtue of his colour he was a 'minority', dumped into the same category as homosexuals.

A bruised ego did not suit Majdy. Instead of humbling him, it turned him sour, made him anxious. In his first term in London, he wrote letters home announcing that he would not make it, threatening that he would give up and return. To call him on the phone, his mother made several trips to the Central Post Office in Khartoum, sat for hours on the low wooden bench fanning her face with the edge of her *tobe* in the stifling heat, shooing away the barefooted children who passed by with loaded trays trying to sell her chewing gum, hairpins, matches. *Get away from my face girl, didn't I just tell you I don't want your gum.*

On the third day she got through, wedged herself into a cubicle and did not close the glass door behind her. His throat tightened when he heard her voice. In the cool corridor of the hostel he held the receiver and leant his head against the wall hiding his face in the crook of his arm. And the students who passed him walked a little bit quicker, felt a little bit awkward hearing his voice heavy with tears, unnaturally loud, his foreign words which they could not understand echoing and hanging around the walls.

There in Khartoum, she also, in her own way, could not understand what he was saying. All this talk about the work being difficult was of course nonsense. Her son was brilliant. Her son always came out top of his class. She had a newspaper photograph of him at sixteen when he got one of the highest marks in the Secondary School Certificate, shaking the now deposed President's hand. His father had slain a sheep for him, distributed the meat among the beggars that slept outside the city's mosque. His sisters had thrown a party for him, heady with singing and dancing. She had circled the pot of burning incense over his head, made him step over it back and forth to ward off the envy and malice that was surely cloaking him. Ninety-nine percent in the math paper, she had ecstatically repeated to friend and relations, Ninety-nine percent and mind you they took that extra mark from him just from sheer miserliness, just so as not to give him the full marks.

Take this thought of coming back out of your mind, she said to him on the long distance line. Repeating it urgently, it was the reason she had called him, the reason she had persisted. Finish your exams and come in the summer, we'll pay the ticket. Don't worry.

They ended up paying for two tickets, his and Sumra's, for when he came in the summer they married. But his mother had known that when she spoke to him on the phone, not with certain knowledge but more like a premonition, a hope.

All his life he had known Sumra, as a cousin of his sister's friend, as the daughter of so-and-so. There was no sudden meeting between them, no childhood romance. He had detached memories of her: a black and white photograph of a child squinting her eyes from the sun, standing with his sister and others in front of the giraffe's cage at the zoo. A teenager in a blue dress and her hair in a single braid, holding a tray of Pepsi bottles at a friend's engagement party. And the horrific story that had fascinated him in his childhood, Sumra getting bitten by a stray dog and having to have thirty rabies injections in her stomach.

In 1985, he had seen her through grape-vines, behind a carport over which the leaves climbed and weaved a criss-crossed maze. He was pressing the bell of a house near the University, in the smaller side roads which housed the University's staff. On the main road, the students were demonstrating against the proposed execution of an opposition party leader. While they were marching for justice, he was searching for Professor Singh, lecturer in Topology, to beg for a reference letter. It was for one of those numerous grants to do post-graduate research that he was always chasing. He could hear the shouting. From where he was it came to him in waves, rising and falling, rhythmic and melodious. He could not make out the exact words, if he had he would have felt his skin prickle against his will, a physical reflex.

They never let the students get very far, they never let them reach the market place where they would swell in numbers, cause a riot. Where other grievances and older pains would join the cry against the injustice of that one death. And deprivation might shake its hypnotic slumber and lash out, snap, in the monotonous heat of the day. Down University Road until the first roundabout and then the teargas would blind them, send them running back, tumbling through the dust, the fallen banners on the ground.

She was crying when she and her friend came running and stood underneath the carport of the house adjacent to the Professor's. Crying from the gas and laughing. *I tore my sandal, it's ruined.* She held it in her hand, the tears running in parentheses down her dust coated face. From all the running her

61

tobe had fallen down, collapsed around her waist and knees, and her hair had escaped the one braid it was tied into and stuck out from her head in triangular spikes. At the nape of her neck, tight little ringlets of hair glistened with sweat, dark and sleek. Laden with moisture, they lay undisturbed and appeared detached from everything else, the teargas and the dust, her torn sandal, her fallen *tobe*. There was a *zeer* in front of the house and he watched her lift the wooden cover, fill the tin mug with water and begin to wash her face. She smoothed her hair with water, searched through it for hair pins which she prised open with her teeth and locked her wayward hair in place.

And all the time she was laughing, crying, sniffing. Chatting to her friend as they both pulled the ends of their *tobes* over their left shoulders, wrapped the material neatly in place and over their hair. *This sandal is so ruined I can't even wear it as a slipper.*

He felt cynical watching them, especially when, now that the demonstration was disbanded, other students passed by, cursing and spitting, with torn shirts and the pathetic remnants of their banners. He did not have the anger to demonstrate, he did not have the ability to enjoy the thrill of rebellion. And the next day, as he predicted, the futility of their action was exposed. The man was hanged, on a Friday morning.

Later, or perhaps at the time he was looking at her through the vines, he thought, I could talk to her now. She would be approachable now, not formal or shy. She would yield to me now. And over the years we would talk of this day again and again and claim it was the start. But he let her go, rang the Professor's bell and soon heard shuffling footsteps coming towards him from inside.

It is pointless to resist fate, impossible to escape its meanderings. But who knows how to distinguish fate's pattern from amidst white noise? Years later when his mother led the campaign My Poor Son All Alone In London Needs A Wife, the name Sumra cropped up. His sister was dispatched to test the waters. The reception was good. Prospective bridegrooms living abroad (it didn't matter where) were in great demand.

Leila Aboulela

When they arrived together in London, he thought that like him she would find it difficult at first and then settle down. Enjoy this clean, civilized life. Be eternally grateful to him for rescuing her from the backwardness of Khartoum. But the opposite happened. During the first months, she showed the enthusiastic approval of the tourist. Enjoyed looking at the shops, was thrilled at how easy all the housework was. She could buy meat already cut up for her. There were all these biscuits and sweets to choose from and they were not expensive at all. Even the pharmacies were stocked so full of medicine in so many different colours and flavours that she almost longed to be ill. Every object she touched was perfect, quality radiated from every little thing. The colour of hairpins did not chip under her nails like it had always done, chewing gum was not the brittle stick that often dissolved in her mouth at the first bite. Empty jam jars were a thing of beauty, she would wash them and dry them and not be able to throw them away. Biscuit tins, those she wanted to collect to take back home, her mother would use to store flour or sugar. Or put her own baked cakes in them, send a tin proudly to the neighbour, and days later the neighbour would return the tin with her own gift inside.

She put on weight, she wrote happy letters home. Majdy showed her the University's library (so many storeys that there are lifts inside and even *toilets*), the shining computer rooms and she was so impressed. She made him feel that he was brilliant, which deep down he knew he was all along. Then the days shortened, became monotonous. She became like the holiday-maker who was getting a little bit too tired of her posh hotel, her exotic surroundings. Everything around her began to feel unreal, temporary, detached from normal real life. Majdy began to talk of getting a work permit when his student visa expired, of not going back after he got his degree.

It was the continuity that she found most alien. It rained and people lifted up umbrellas and went their way, the shelves in the supermarket would empty and fill again. The milkman delivered milk everyday.

Don't your lectures ever get cancelled? Don't your lecturers

63

get ill, don't their wives give birth? When the Queen dies, will they give everyone a holiday?

She'll die on a Sunday, he would say laughing at her questions. This is what civilisation is, the security to build your life, to make something out of it. Not to be hindered all the time by coups and new laws, by sitting all day in a petrol queue. By not being able to get your ill child to a doctor because they are on strike.

She listened carefully to everything he said. Would nod in agreement though her eyes remained wary. When she spoke of the future though, she would imagine they were going back, as if his hopes of staying in London were only dreams, or as if his hopes were an inevitability she wished to deny. I imagine you coming home at two, she would say, there would not be this endlessly long working day like here.

We would sleep in the afternoon under the fan, its blades a grey blur, the sun so hard and bright that it would still be with us through the closed shutters. I would tease you about your students, are the girls pretty, do they come to your office after lectures and sweetly say Ustaz, I can't understand this, I can't understand that. Ustaz, don't be so hard on us when you're marking our exam. And you would laugh at me and shake your head, say I'm talking rubbish but I would know from your eyes how much my possessiveness pleasures you. The children playing on the roof would wake us up, their footsteps thudding over the hum of the fan. They are not allowed up there, it is not safe among the jagged green pieces of glass that ward off thieves. And you are furious with them, you go outside and throw your slipper at your son as he drops himself down from the tree, one foot balanced on the window sill. He is the eldest, the instigator. But he is mischievous and ducks, you miss him and have to shout BRING THE SLIPPER BACK. From inside I hear his laugh like cool tumbling water. You once bought a whip for this boy, you got it from the souk in Omdurman where they sell good whips and you were quite pleased with yourself that day. You lashed it through the air to frighten the children with its snake-like power. But you did not have much of a chance to use it because he took it and threw it on top of the neighbour's roof and so it remained there among the fluffs of dust, razor blades and other things the wind carried to that roof. I would make tea with mint. By now the sun would have nearly set, it would be the hottest part of the day, no breeze, no movement, as if the whole world was holding its breath for the departure of the sun. Our neighbour comes over and you drink the tea together, he brings with him the latest gossip, another political fiasco and you are amused, your good mood is restored. Your son behaves well in front of guests, he leaves his play, comes and shakes the man's hand. The sound of grief cuts the stillness of the evening, like a group of birds howling, circling, yapping with their throats. The wail of death. We guess it must be the elderly neighbour across the square, he has been in and out of hospital for some time. I grab my *tobe* and run, run in my slippers to mourn with them.

You are hallucinating, woman. This is Majdy's answer. He has proof. Number one, I will never, with the salary the University pays its lecturers, be able to afford us a house or a flat of our own. Unless I steal or accept bribes and there is not much opportunity for either in my kind of work. We would probably live with my parents, my mother would get on your nerves sooner or later. You will complain of her day and night and you will be angry with me because you expect me to take your side and I don't. Number two, how will I ever get to the souk of Omdurman with no petrol and there is unlikely to be any electricity for your fan. The last thing, why do you assume that nothing pleases me better than drinking tea and gossiping with the neighbour? This is exactly the kind of waste of time that I want to get away from. That whole atmosphere where so-called intellectuals spend their time arguing about politics. Every lecturer defined by his political beliefs, every promotion would depend on one's political inclination and not the amount of research he's done, the papers he's published. My colleagues would be imagining that it is their responsibility to run the country. Debating every little thing from every abstract angle. The British gave it up, packed and left without putting up a fight and somehow the Sudanese carry this air of pride, of belief that their large, crazy country will one day rise gracefully from its backwardness and yield something good!

She sometimes argued back when he spoke like that. Accused him of disloyalty, a lack of feeling. Sometimes she would be silent for days, control herself and not mention either the future or the past. Then like one breaking a fast, she would speak, offer him memories and stories, wait for him to take them. Wait with the same patience, the same serene insistence with which the little girls in the Central Post Office had offered pins and gum to his mother.

President Sadat of Egypt came to visit Khartoum and all the schools were let out early so that the children could line the streets. The sudden announcement from the teacher that there would be no more lessons today, that wild feeling of being unleashed, let loose in the streets to buy *dandurma* and suck the mango ice from the hole in the little plastic bag. Then standing in her blue uniform and white *tarha* with her friends all along Airport Road, its lampposts decked with the flags of Egypt and the Sudan, shouting themselves hoarse to welcome the President in his gleaming limousine.

Rain that made silver puddles. The sun disappearing for a day, the new smell of the earth. And there would be no work that day, no school. The cars stranded islands in the flooded streets.

Because there are no proper gutters, he would tell her. No drainage system and all those potholes. Remember the stink of the stagnant water days later. The mosquitoes that would descend spreading disease.

Silver puddles, she would say, shimmering under a sky strange with blue clouds.

Another memory, she offers it like a flower pressed shyly into his hands. On the week before they came to London, they went to visit his uncle. The electricity cut and the air cooler's roar turned to a purr, its fan flapped and then all the sound died down. The sudden darkness, the sudden silence. They sat and listened to the gentle drip drop sound of the water on the air cooler's fresh straw. Opened the windows to let in the faint night air and the scents from the jasmine bushes. Moonlight filled the room with

66

blue-grey shadows. Outlines rose of the coloured sweets on the table, the ice melting in their glasses of lemon juice. While their hosts stumbled around in search of candles and lights, he held her hand stroking each of her fingers with his thumb.

But Sumra, don't I hold your hand here, he would ask, gentle with her now. Do you want a power cut in London? Think of that: elevators, traffic lights, the trains. Chaos and fear. They would write about it in the newspapers, talk about in on TV. And in Khartoum it is an everyday event, another inconvenience, part of the misery of life. Defrosted fridges become cupboards, the food soggy and rotting inside.

Sometimes he looked at her and felt compassion. Felt that yes, she did not belong here. Looked at the little curls at the nape of her neck, dry now and light, not moist with sweat and thought that she was meant for lingering sunsets and thin cotton dresses. Her small teeth made to strip the hard husk of sugar cane, her dimples for friends and neighbours. He could see her in idle conversation, weaving the strands of gossip with a friend. Passing the time among the shades of palm trees and bougainvillaeas, in a place where the hours were long.

Most times though, he could not understand how she was not excited by the opportunities their new life held. How she could not admire the civilized way that people went about their business here, the efficient post that arrived on time, ambulances and fire engines that never let anyone down. The way a cheque card can slide through a wedge on the wall and crisp cash emerge. These impressed her, but not for long. She exclaimed at how the pigeons and ducks in the parks were left unmolested. No one captured them to eat them. But instead of enjoying their beauty she brooded on how poor her own people were.

He began to think of her homesickness as perverse. Her reluctance to wholeheartedly embrace their new life, an intransigence. He began to feel bored by her nostalgia, her inability to change, to initiate a new life for herself. He had in the time he had spent in London met Sudanese and Arab women who seemed to blossom in their new surroundings. He had seen them in tight

67

trousers they would not dare wear back home, playing with lighted cigarettes in their hands. Delighting in that simple action, something they could not do back home because it was considered unbecoming for a woman to smoke in public, yet here no one cared. And though he did not expect her or really want her to do exactly these same things, he was disappointed that she did not capture that same spirit and instead seemed shyer, more reserved than she ever was in Khartoum. She wanted to wear her *tobe,* cover her hair and he would say no, no, not here, I do not want us to be associated with backwardness.

It is frightening to come home at the end of the day and find your wife sitting, just sitting in her dressing gown and her hair uncombed just as you have left her in the morning. She, who checks her reflection in every mirror, who for you scents her hair with sandalwood, dips steel in kohl to wipe the rims of her eyes. You find her sitting and the whole place is untouched, no smells of cooking, the bed unmade, mugs stained with tea, the remaining few flakes of cereal swollen in their bowl. She is silent, looks at you as if you didn't exist, does not yield or soften under your touch. Stroke her hair and rub her hands and probe for the right words, the words she wants to hear. Talk of jasmine-scented gardens, of a wedding dance, of the high Nile breaking its banks. Until she can cry.

For days afterwards, as he put his key in the lock, as he turned it, he would brace himself for that same scene, he would fear a reoccurrence. He had been happy that day. While she sat at home with a frozen heart, he had glimpsed a modest success, a slight break-through in his work. A paper he had been looking for, a paper written five years ago in his same area of work was located in another library. And he had gone there, to that college on the other side of London, an event in itself, for he was always at the library or using the Mainframe computers. He had found it, photocopied it, warmed to its familiar notation and travelled back, full of gratitude, appreciation for that meticulous body of knowledge, the technology that enabled one to locate written material. We are centuries behind, he would tell her later, in things like that we are too far behind to ever catch up. And while she had sat in her dressing gown, immobile, ignoring hunger and thirst, he had entered the mind of that other mathematician, followed his logic and when finding an error (the subscript for lambda should have been t-1 and not t), a typing error or a more serious slip from the writer, he had been infused with a sense of pleasure. So that even while he knelt next to her and asked, what is wrong, what has happened, the formulae with their phis and gammas and lambdas still frolicked in his brain and the idea occurred to him that her name, if he ignored its real Arabic meaning, sounded just like these Greek letters, these enigmatic variables with their soft shapes and gentle curves. Alpha, lambda, sigma, beta, Sumra.

He proposed a practical solution to her problem. She must do something with herself, she was too idle, and as she was not allowed to work without a permit then she must study, do a course or something. Word processing; she could then type his thesis for him. He was enthusiastic about the idea, a word processing course of a few weeks and through it perhaps she would meet others like herself from all over the world, make friends, keep busy. So she, who had once braved teargas, the crush of running feet, now faces a middle-aged teacher, a jolly woman who travels to Tunisia for her holidays, comes back encased in kaftans and a chequered scarf around her shoulders. Who gushes at her and says, you must be so relieved that you are here, all that war and famine back home. You must be so glad that you are not there now. Those poor children, and she gives a shudder then of her fine plump shoulders, a tremble of her cheeks, eyelids drooping. Clasps her hands so that the coloured stones on her rings grind in pain and says, I can't bear to see these innocent children on TV. From such a woman she recoils in fear as if she was not the same girl he had seen long ago who laughed and held a torn sandal in her hand.

Out of exasperation or pity, he suggested that she should go home for a few months. He winced as he saw her try to hide the eagerness from her voice when she said yes, that would be nice. And the polite questions, wouldn't the ticket be too expensive, would he be all right on his own? Then she left, easily, so easily as if she had never truly arrived, never laid down roots that needed pulling out.

While she was away, London became more familiar to him. He thought of it as his new home and it was as if the city responded. He could feel it softening around him, becoming genial in its old age. The summers getting hotter and hotter. A new humid heat, sticky, unlike the dry burning of the desert he had left behind. People filled the streets, the parks, a population explosion or as if a season of imprisonment was over and they were now free. They lay immobile on towels spread on the grass, drove in cars without roofs, spilt out of cafes onto the pavements.

Beggars squatted around the stations, Third World style. The sight of the beggars jarred him, he could not look them in the face, he could not give them money. He had a faint memory of discovering that in advanced countries begging was illegal. The information, incredible to him and awe-inspiring, had been in his mind part of the magic of the western world. A place where everyone's livelihood was so guaranteed that begging could be considered a crime.

He had once told Sumra that this country chips away one's faith, but he began to see that it chipped away indiscriminately at all faith, even faith in itself. And as it accepted him, his admiration for it decreased, his faith in it wavered. It was no longer enough, as it once had been, that he was here, that he was privileged to walk London's streets, smell the books of its libraries, feast his eyes on its new, shining cars. He would walk on wet roads that never flooded and realize that he would never know what it would be like to say *my ancestors built this, my grandfather borrowed a book from this library*. The city held something that could never be his, that was impossible to aspire to.

Through the summer, he slowly lost his sense of awe and he marvelled at how quickly one could take things for granted, a proof of man's ability to adapt. Yet it was sad, the unredeemable loss of wonder. He began to expect and not be amazed that the library opened every day, that when a printer broke down it was fixed, that the software would be updated regularly. He could no longer sustain the gratitude he used to feel and as awe slipped away nothing rose to take its place but silence.

The silence made him pause and notice things that would not have caught his attention before. In Bath, where he went for a two-day conference, he watched his supervisor, a professor eminent in his field whom he admired greatly, ask a colleague for some change for the coffee machine. He watched the two men, elderly with greying hair, with textbooks and papers in their own names, exchange the coins. Watched his supervisor put in his colleague's outstretched hand the exact coins, ten, fifteen, seventeen, nineteen and here's a penny. Every coin was a pulse of disappointment to Majdy and he wondered how two men who possessed all the prerequisites for dignity could be limited, incapable of largesse. Yet was not this a side of the efficiency he so admired, the individuality he considered modern?

In the silence, he would hear Sumra's voice. I am not making this up, she had said one night as they walked in a side street sleek with rain and yellow lamplight. This really happened, she had said and held his hand because the street, though lined with parked cars, was empty of people.

A woman, an elderly woman your mother's age, was on her way to visit a friend whose sister had died. She stood an hour waiting for a bus. None came; transport was bad that day because of the petrol shortage. The sun burnt her head, she was not used to going out of the house, she was exhausted from standing. She walked to the middle of the road, stood right in the middle of the road and raised her hand, palm upwards. She stopped the first car, opened the front door and got in. My son, she said to the driver, I am fed up of waiting for transport. And I can't move another step. For Allah's sake, drive me to my friend, I'll show you the way there. Her sister died four days ago and I still haven't been to see her. He drove her there even though it wasn't on his way, what could he have done? And all the way, as they chatted, he called her Aunt.

When Sumra had told him this story, he had answered with a tirade against the exaggerated importance of mourning among the

Sudanese. The days that were wasted, the pique if friends or relations did not come to mourn, or did not come often enough. Yet on those summer nights when the delayed sunlight distracted him from work, and Sumra was not there to help him study late into the night as she used to do with her presence, the click of the spoon as she stirred sugar in tea, the chiming of her bracelets, he would hear her voice and not remember very clearly the words he had used to answer her.